W9-AFA-804

ANIMALS
Black and White

Phyllis Limbacher Tildes

Charlesbridge

I gallop gracefully on the grassy plains of Africa.

The lion is my worst enemy.

What am I?

a zebra

I love to graze on sweet grasses. I travel with a large herd for protection from predators.

My large fins and
flippers make me look
like a huge fish as I
surge through
the water.

But I'm a mammal,
just like you.

What am I?

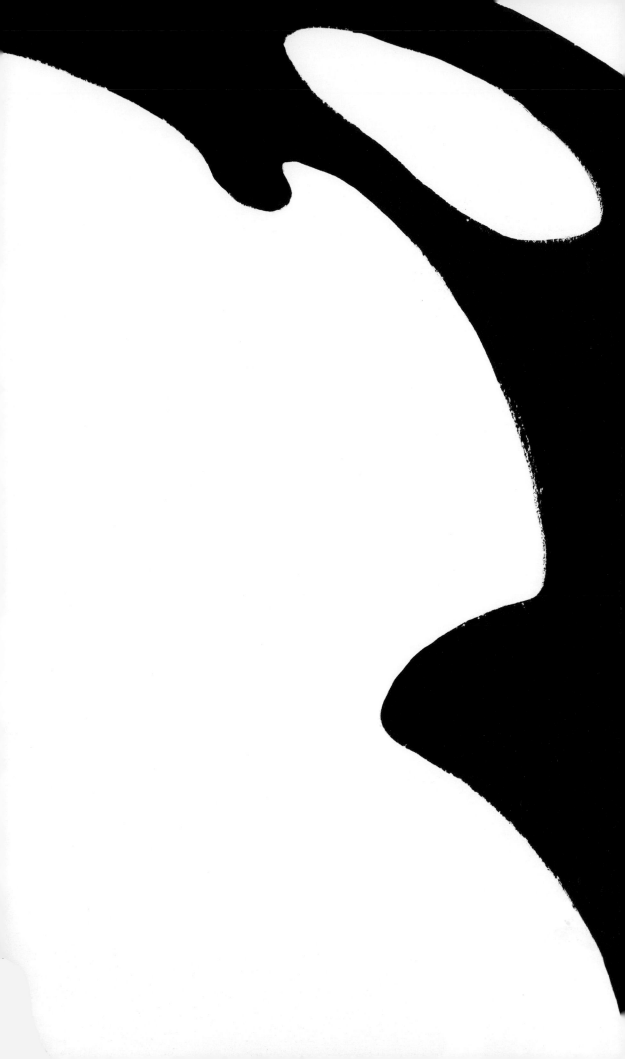

an orca

I am a large dolphin, but I'm
also called a *killer whale*.
I roam the ocean, hunting
with up to fifty of my friends.

I live in the misty mountains far, far to the east. I love to chew bamboo.

What am I?

a giant panda

I like to nap in trees
in the hidden mountain
forests of central China.
I am very rare.

I swim on the glassy surface of a lake. I dive into the deep, dark water for fish.

I have a sad, lonely call.

What am I?

a loon

I'm heavy and ride
low in the water.

When I want to fly,
I need a large lake to
get a running start.

See how my baby chick likes to ride on my back.

I wander through the woods at night. My wide, striped tail sweeps the ground. When I meet trouble, I lift my tail like a warning flag.

What am I?

a skunk

I'm usually quite shy, but if I need to, I can stop my enemies with a smelly, stinging spray.

I teach my hungry babies to look for beetles, grubs, and mice.

I am a bird. I "fly" gracefully beneath the cold, blue waters of the ocean.

But when I'm on land, I waddle like a very clumsy duck.

What am I?

a penguin

I can swim for days
in icy water looking for
fish, shrimp, and squid.

I take turns with my
mate minding our
young chicks in the
rocky rookery.

I flit and flutter from flower to flower in search of sweet nectar.

Although my wings look like tissue paper, they are strong enough to fly miles and miles!

What am I?

a butterfly

I am an *African mocker swallowtail*. I once was a fat caterpillar, munching on crisp, green leaves.

After a long sleep in my chrysalis, I became a butterfly.

Did you know?

 The **zebra** is a tiger-striped relative of the horse. There are many kinds of zebras in Africa. They vary in size and in the pattern of their stripes. Zebras travel in large herds of their own kind and sometimes with other animals such as giraffes, wildebeests, and ostriches. The zebra's keen sense of hearing helps alert other herd members to predators. Its stripes provide camouflage at twilight when lions are hunting.

 The **orca** is the fastest whale and largest dolphin in existence. It can grow up to thirty feet long and weigh up to nine tons. It prefers to hunt in a group, or school, in coastal waters in search of large fish, penguins, sea lions, and other whales. Although it is also known as the killer whale, it is a gentle and affectionate mate, often sharing its food even in captivity. It communicates with its musical calls. Family units remain together for a long time. The orca is also very curious. It likes to swim close to boats—but there has never been a report of an orca intentionally attacking a human.

 The **giant panda** looks like a cuddly, roly-poly bear with its large, round face, thick fur, and wobbly walk. Although it is playful, the panda is also quite shy, living alone in the remote forests of central China. It is one of the world's rarest endangered animals. The panda spends most of the day eating up to eighty pounds of bamboo, gripping the stalks with its five fingers and thumblike sixth digit. Baby pandas do not begin to eat bamboo until they are about a year old. Before then, the mother provides rich milk for her baby. A panda lives about twenty-two years and can grow to be three hundred pounds.

The ***common loon*** is a powerful swimmer. Its webbed feet are set far back on its body, making it difficult for the loon to walk on land. It nests on the inland lakes and ponds of North America. The loon mates for life and is a devoted parent. The parents take turns tending the nest of two dark brown eggs. Newborn chicks quickly take to the water, floating like fluffy, bobbing corks. A lucky loon will live for twenty to thirty years. The saying "crazy as a loon" comes from the loon's laughterlike call, which echoes across a lonely lake.

The ***striped skunk*** is a cat-sized animal related to the weasel family. It lives in the woods throughout most of North America. It has a triangle-shaped head, a pointed nose, and sharp claws that are helpful for digging. At night the striped skunk follows fence rows and the bushy border of the woods in search of insects, seeds, berries, eggs, and mice. When a skunk meets a possible attacker, it will stamp its feet in warning before squirting its awful-smelling spray ten feet or more. Even four-week-old skunks are equipped with this weapon.

The ***Adélie penguin*** looks like a comical little man in a tuxedo. However, it is better adapted than a human being to survive in the Antarctic. A penguin has a thick layer of fat to protect it from severe cold. Its feathers provide a smooth surface, helping its streamlined body glide through water. Unlike other birds, the penguin has solid bones that help it dive. It can toboggan over ice on its belly, using its flipperlike wings to propel itself. Penguin parents raise their young in huge nesting colonies called rookeries.

The ***African mocker swallowtail*** butterfly and other swallowtails are big and beautiful. The largest ones have wingspans of up to six inches, and most have a tail on each hind wing. Swallowtail caterpillars emit a strong smell when they are annoyed. The *African mocker swallowtail* has a black-and-white pattern, but other swallowtails come in many colors. Butterflies are creatures of the daytime, preferring to fly only in sunshine. Most butterflies live four to six weeks, some only a few days.

For my sister, Sandra,
with love

With special thanks to my editor, Juliana McIntyre
— P. L. T.

Published by Charlesbridge Publishing
85 Main Street, Watertown, MA 02172-4411
(617) 926-0329

Library of Congress Cataloging-in-Publication Data
Tildes, Phyllis Limbacher.
Animals: black and white / Phyllis Limbacher Tildes.
p. cm.
Summary: While one page presents specific information which serves
as a clue to the identity of a particular black-and-white animal, the next
page reveals the name of the animal.
ISBN 0-88106-960-4 (trade hardcover)
ISBN 0-88106-961-2 (library reinforced)
ISBN 0-88106-959-0 (softcover)
1. Animals—Juvenile literature.
2. Animals—Identification—Juvenile literature.
3. Color of animals—Juvenile literature.
[1. Animals. 2. Color of animals.] I. Title.
QL49.T425 1996
591—dc20   96-948

Printed in China
(hc) 10 9 8 7 6 5 4 3 2 1
(sc) 10 9 8 7 6 5 4 3 2 1

The illustrations in this book were done in gouache on Strathmore
3-ply illustration paper, kid finish.
The display type and text type were set in Impact and Veljovic.
Color separations were made by Pure Imaging, Watertown, Massachusetts.
Printed and bound by Palace Press International
Production supervision by Brian G. Walker
Designed by Phyllis L. Tildes and Beth Santos